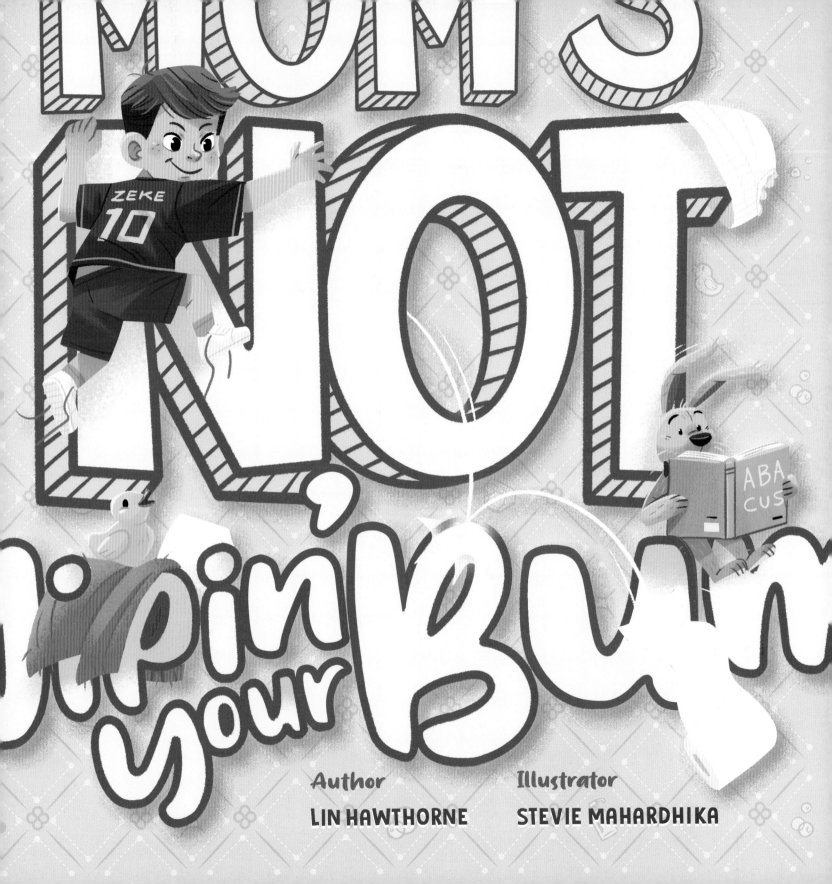

MOM'S NOT FLIPIN' YOUR BUN

Author
LIN HAWTHORNE

Illustrator
STEVIE MAHARDHIKA

Name: _____

ze ke

I will wipemyownb

I will wipemyo

I will wipemyown

Hey Ab, will you don

clean fannies are fu

clean fannies are fun

clean fannies are fu

To Joshua, Samuel, TJ, and Rachel
and Wynter B.
And especially "Uncle Bum"

–LH

For my daughter

–SM

Book ONE in the Mom's Not® Book Series
A Grow With Me® Book

MOM'S NOT Wipin' Your Bum

Three Plus One Publishing™
PHOENIX

Author

LIN HAWTHORNE

Illustrator

STEVIE MAHARDHIKA

Now that you're big,
(much bigger than small),

there's
something
you're ready
to know.

Your diapers are done, and clean fannies are fun!

BUT...

Your gifts—stinkin' cute.

Yes... even
your toots.

But Mommy has HAD IT with poo.
A "front to back" sweep

Remember this game?

"Come back!"
I would say.

We would race ten times a day!

We changed for the better.
Bye, saggy old diaper!

Now dry through the day,
you take breaks when we play.

Run to the potty and GO!

Just roll up some tissue
and take care of the issue.

When your bathroom

is smellin' upstairs

and you're yellin',

"HEY, MOM!"

First, try a neat feat on your bottom's top seat!

So many things new–
a challenge or two.

STEPS OF CHILDHOOD

CRAWLING

RIDING BIKE

STANDING ON HEAD

EATING ICE CREAM

The potty's the
biggest one yet!

Flying germs
through the air?

Never fear,
almost there!

Flush, wash, then hang ten. You wiped your **OWN** bum... and AMEN!

YOU'RE DONE IN A SNAP!

Now Mom needs a nap.